Letters Undelivered

Lianne Figueroa

Letters Undelivered

Dedicated to all women who love too hard, and care too much.
To those who have experienced love, but could not keep it.
No matter what you go through in life, just know, you are not alone.

This is for you —

Contents

Self-Love

I have learned the hard way
that looking for love
will not help me find it,
but that does not give me
an excuse to quit.

Falling in love with yourself is essential;
it's not something confidential.

So we'll make countless mistakes
until we figure out
that loving ourselves first
is what life is all about.

And all that comes after is a plus,
but the love we show ourselves is a must.

- L. Figueroa

Daddy's Girl

My father warned me about boys, when I was young.
He said they'll always lie, and say *"You're The One"*.
But be careful baby girl, it's just some lies and tricks,
to get a quick fix. You must control your emotions, he said.
Don't let them get to your head. You're strong, little one.
Don't let them take your heart and run.
Remember, those boys are not too bright.
They've just got your body in sight.

I see it dad, I understand it *now*.
You warned me way before I could understand how.
You warned me that love breaks your heart when you
don't see it coming. But I was so young then.

Dad please come pick me up, fix my heart, and stitch it up.
I don't want to love these foolish boys anymore.
I promise, Daddy I'm sure!
But princess he says, "Only you
can cut any hanging threads".

I raised a smart girl he tells me, while I lay down to sleep.
"I believe in you, and I wouldn't tell you if it wasn't true,
remember that I love you, and you'll always make it through".

- L. Figueroa

Have a good one.

I prayed for you today because I miss you, as much as I don't want to.
I couldn't ever wish anything bad upon you.
That would be too easy, that would be too weak of me.

Instead, I wish you guidance. I wish that you
remember how much I love you, and how much
I meant it when I said I'll always have your back.

I wish you could take a lot of what you did, **back**.

I have such a hard time accepting that I can't control certain situations.
If it were up to me, there would be nothing short of appreciation for
everything we used to bring to the table. But we are no longer *able* to make
amends for our mistakes because what's done is done, and it'd be **too** late.

However, that does not erase the memories, and I'm not certain that I want
them gone when they're all that I have left to reminisce on. 'Cause there's no
more pictures, and your belongings have been thrown away.
I remember when I *never* thought I'd see the day.
Either way, I prayed for you today.

- L. Figueroa

A Mess Of Love

It's clear that I deserve a better love, a king for *one*.
Telling myself to let go, knowing it's easier said than done.
What do I want from you? I'm not even sure.
Got me feeling so insecure; praying for God to send me a cure for the
mess, I obsess about. You fill my heart with so much *doubt* that
anyone could ever love someone like me,
because what I want from you could *never* be.
But my heart is still pure, and it's my love you endure.
Leaving me broken, with so many words unspoken
but all you hear is drama and headaches, I just don't get it.
Now lie and say you still care about me too,
I dare you.

- L. Figueroa

July

I fell in love with your disguise.
A good looking face, and those intriguing eyes.
But it's that same face I now despise.
You faked the front so well, I just
couldn't tell, and that's how I fell.
Why didn't you pick me up?
Said you would *never* give me up.
You fooled me babe, & you're not
nearly as ashamed as me, even though
you should be. But I'm embarrassed for
loving a person who was not meant to
experience a dream so vivid.
You've left me livid.
I've fallen out of love with you, but it's so sad
that I will always miss what we once had.

- *L. Figueroa*

Save it

I guess I never really can win,
since you're the type to leave
then reel me back in.
How dare you play with my emotions?
Like I mean nothing to you,
I'm getting really sick of you.

But I can't change my number
because then I'll always wonder
what you had to tell me. Little
things like that, still matter to me.
And you keep tabs, I could tell.
But for what? You said you don't dwell.
On her... you said you're done.
Yet, she's still claiming you're *the one*.

I'd just love to ask why I ever had to be involved.
There's nothing worse than a relationship unresolved.
And extended invitations to an uninviting party.

Yeah, I know I know... you're so sorry.

Save it.

- L. Figueroa

Forgive My Lying Eyes

I have to applaud your persistence,
on fucking up then asking for forgiveness --
You begged me time and time again to let it go,
you said there were a lot of things you didn't know.
Whatever that was about, I gave you the benefit of the doubt.
But that never meant loving you, the same way I used to.

I will never love that hard again,
I will never give you that much emotion.
I forgave you for the way you acted,
and the things you said.
I forgave you for the lies you spread.
But those memories will never leave my head.

I loved you when no one else did,
hoping you'd wake up, but God forbid.
You never believed in anything
if it did not benefit you, and
I'm supposed to believe in you?

- L. Figueroa

I Told You

I tell myself I need space,
but then I end up on this route back to your place.
I tell myself it won't be the same, but nothing has changed. I can't
even tell who's to blame.
It's this game, and I can't quit. I have to admit, it has me sick.
With all these preconceived notions; words go unspoken.
I feel like I'm choking.
I ask myself, *"Why do I want this?"*
I guess ignorance really is bliss.
Just lay here, and give me one last kiss.
I told you I won't be here for long,
but you only hear me when I point out your wrongs.
Why can't you see the love in me, and let it change your ways?
You know we've seen better days.
I can tell that you feel this way too,
so I guess I'll just wait...on you.

- L. Figueroa

For My Mother

Too much love - you give.
Too much heart - you hold.
Still, your smile shines like gold.

Too many tears - you've shed.
Too many open wounds - from which you've bled.
But you continue to love - instead.

Too much for them,
not enough for you.
I just wonder when you'll be
enough for you.
And if you'll ever realize how much
I love you.

- L. Figueroa

Shaking My Head

I've forgotten what it's like to trust, without the fear of betrayal.
I never learned how to be in a relationship, thinking it won't fail.
These issues do not come from my experiences only.
See, I've heard stories.

So many women have been broken,
allowing things they did not deserve.
There's a lot that I've observed.

But do you know how painful it is
to not be able to fix this?

Do you know how many women have been emotionally abused,
and taken for granted, being lied to, and left confused?
With similar hearts and intelligent minds,
and spines stronger than mine.

I've been taught lessons by women of all ages,
from all types of generations. Most of them
have agreed that I should never get married.

I should be content with my single life,
and never strive to just be a wife.
They've all said that love is not the same
in a relationship, once each partner says "I do".
I did not believe this at first, but I've seen it, *it's true.*

I've seen more tears than lasting years, and I have
empathized with these poor souls.
I've given advice like nobody knows.
But do you know what it's like
to lose faith in the concept of love,
and associate it with being taken advantage of?
Can you imagine the fear instilled in me,
or why I might never want the opportunity?

They said to be the change you want to see,
but nobody has changed for me.

- L. Figueroa

Profound Lovers

They like to call me "**crazy**"
Because I love hard.
I think it's called strength,
maybe awareness.
I know exactly who, and what
will hurt me.
But, I still love with all my heart.
Crazy right?

- L. Figueroa

Make A Wish

When I look at you, it only takes me a few
to remember why we didn't work out.
I remember how much I loved you,
up until I found out
all the ways you did me wrong,
meanwhile everyone knew
we wouldn't last long.
I was running around defending you,
while you were busy spreading
lies that weren't true.

Rumors about us, and the things I did.
While I was busy dreaming of a marriage and kids.
You didn't protect me or any of the things we built.

Yet even after all the shame, tears, and guilt,
I want nothing but the best for you in this lifetime,
I'm just done wishing you were *mine*.

- *L. Figueroa*

What is true at twenty-two

Let's get something straight in the meantime,
I *never* broke anyone's heart who hadn't already broken mine.

You said that you can't be my lover,
but you also can't stand to see me with another.
And now, you think we should wait for each other?
Meanwhile, all these girls keep blowing your cover.

So let me take a minute to remind you,
that I know a few guys who
are truly into me.
Asking me sincerely,
for my time and energy
plus all I can't provide
because I've lost my sense of clarity.
And this distance between you & I
just isn't fair to me. Yet arguing
is the only option you see?

And silent treatments say more than
one hundred word vents,
but neither one will make amends.
So neither one of us presses send,
back to square one yet again.

- L. Figueroa

3:14 am

I could have asked you how your day
had been, a little more often.
I could have told you why
I blew things out of proportion
instead of driving you
straight into exhaustion.
I could have told you
that I wanted more with you,
but I didn't know it *then*.

I picked up your energy
and knew we wouldn't last.
I couldn't explain much if you asked;
you just remind me so much of my past.
But there's something about your style,
and the way I make you smile.
It hasn't felt this enticing in a while.

Some days you act really good, only
when you want to be understood.
But I can't keep up with your moods,
better yet – your moves,
and what they all include.

And as for you,
you won't allow yourself to be
the man that I need. So what's left?
A couple cute texts.
and another night or two?…
Damn I got Déjà vu.

- L. Figueroa

Personal

I must be crazy, or too nice,
to let you back in on my life.
Allowing you to see how I'm doing;
do you know how much of me you ruined?

You took, with you, some of the best parts of me.
Some of the parts a lot of people won't get to see.
I could never be the way I used to be.
So loving of everyone who leaves.

But I think in spite of all of that
knowing everything I know,
it's okay that I let it go.
And remind you of how bright
my light shines, and how sharp
I like my rhymes. Don't ever front,
like you don't know who I am.
At one point you were telling everyone
"I Love Lianne".

- L. Figueroa

Lost

I reminisce on all the beginnings with you,

I followed you into a new world.

Uncertain of my surroundings,

I let you take me in deeper.

I trusted your lead,

& hoped my tomorrows would end with you.

You changed on me.

I thought you were my safety.

Steady chasing memories,

while you abandoned me.

Now you've got me lost.

- L. Figueroa

Same Old Fling

I know they still ask
"What's the deal with you and her?"
"Are you still dealing with her?"
But you're always smoking, so it's all a blur.
Just don't ever tell them our secrets,
& don't let them into your head.
No one else has to know what happened in my bed.
But after it's all been said and done,
I just hope I was your *favorite* one.

- L. Figueroa

Blue Dream

The same guy who set the bar so high for everyone else,
can't even seem to follow the standards he set, himself.

Laziness *
such an ugly character trait that you've obtained.
I can't even look at you the same.

The excitement has died down,
and neither one of us makes a sound,
until the rush of your lips against my hips
becomes another night full of passion and regret.
Yet, the foundation of our bodies *together*
formulates the most beautiful silhouette,
not sure how you could ever seem to forget.

I was once your queen, and you aspired to give me
the world on a silver platter, and now? None of it matters.
But I cannot deny that you did set the bar high,
and so my standards will remain strong,
until my next king comes along.

- L. Figueroa

She said ;

I decided to paint my own picture of him,
I focused on the side he held within.
I couldn't accept who he was meant to be,
I wanted to believe he was made for just *me*.
I guess my heart sees what it wants to see.

Why has love made me so blind?
Why have I only ever loved one *kind* of man?
The kind that doesn't plan to stay;
the kind that always lets temptation get in the way.
The kind that starts to express feelings, then runs away.

I'm sick and tired of only knowing one type of love,
I want the kind I've always dreamed of.
When will I find the answers to my questions?
Haven't I learned enough damn lessons?
And if I am not meant to fix these men,
why do they insist on having me then?

They all seem to be broken, lost, and
confused passing along all their issues.
Yet, I can't seem to turn them away, always
hoping I'll make a lover out of them *someday*.

- *L. Figueroa*

This Too Shall Pass

I could tell that there will always be something missing.
There's something about the way you touch me, while we're kissing.
It's far from exciting, and a little less than inviting,
but I still find myself writing out these texts to you;
wondering who exactly is next to you.

Actually I'm busy wondering, whose got the best of you,
and is it true that its not over between you two.
You've got me feeling like the attention
you show me is so damn phony.
You're probably only entertaining *this* out of loneliness.
I could tell your ex haunts you late at night, and it's not right.
There's no need to lie. She's always on your brain,
otherwise you would refrain to mix up our names.

There's no need for apologies,
Man, it doesn't even bother me.
I've got a history of my own,
and I've already had my time alone.

So I'll never settle for a competition.

Especially if I'm not even the one you're missing.

I never needed the lies in disguise as protection,

I already knew the truth, so no need to stress it.

Just wish I could fathom the reality of that connection.

Yet, in my mind, it just won't seem to register.

I mean, how could you ever compare me to *her*?

But whatever, right?

Have fun with your mistress.

After all, it's no longer any of my business.

- L. Figueroa

4 Year Anniversary

Anxiously waiting, but scared to hear the truth.
What is she about to tell you?
You reassure her, you've done *nothing* wrong,
so then why are you so worried?
The guilt is haunting you.
It has become a little reckless.
Your legs shake, and your hands tremble
as your thoughts begin to unravel.
You know there is a missing piece to this mystery.
You thought you left it in the past, you thought it was history.
But you left the door opened, and your secret is lingering.
She looks up at you and says,
"I know you've been cheating".

- L. Figueroa

You Will Never Know

Pretty little woman with a heart of gold,
can't seem to remember when the world got this cold.

Such a good girl in search of all the things she can't seem to find.
All of these men admiring her grind, but they just like to waste her
time. Trying her with the same pickup lines.

Yet, she waits on you, with no peace of mind.

Love is blind, but maybe lust is worse,
addicted to your empty promises?
Man, she's **cursed**.
Bet you never stop to think
about how much her heart *hurts*.

And the minute she tries drifting away,
you never forget to remind her
how it's *you* that's not okay.
But when she asks you to stay,
you've got nothing left to say.

Trying to recognize the blessings of each new day,
but this mess stays on her mind anyway.

- L. Figueroa

29

Moving On

You say you need time, some peace of mind.
So selfish it seems, but I know what you mean.
It's a little sad that I've come to find, there is *nothing*
special about you being mine. You're just someone
I chose to waste my time with, now that I think it over.
I'm done looking over your shoulder, you've gotten colder.
We will never see eye to eye, you'll always be partially blind.
My love, maybe one day we will cross each other's paths.
Maybe even share some laughs, but you'll know that
you missed out on something great, as you watch me
walk off with my new date. You'll think, "Damn if only
she were mine again", "I'd give anything to make her grin".
But she is a Queen who deserves a throne,
and it's no surprise because *you should have known.*

- L. Figueroa

Relief

In the mornings, I would make your bed for you.
I would fold your clothes and clean whatever I could,
to leave a smile on your face when you returned.
Some mornings, I would even wait for you,
when I should have made time for more important things.

Some mornings, I hoped you wouldn't be too long.
I wanted to give you one more kiss, and one last hug
in hopes that you would ask me to stay longer.

This morning, I woke up and made my bed.
I folded my clothes, and cleaned whatever I could.
I thought of you, and I smiled. I hope you're doing well.
This morning, I made time for myself, so don't wait for me.

- L. Figueroa

Eye Candy

He is so beautiful, and he doesn't even know it.
My eyes feed into his every move
though I try not to show it.
I admire his thoughts, his words.
Tell me more. *I'm yours.*
I could never deny that what I feel
for him is worth a million words.
But my pride is much too strong
to let him string me along.
Yet he is all that I desire,
without warning
his attention gets me higher.
Higher than I have ever been,
no way I could let anyone else in.
To want all of him, in this way,
should be a *sin.*
Even then, I would ask for constant forgiveness,
no matter how reckless our love gets.
But he and I were never meant to be,
this was never planned, until he took my hand.
He loved me, he said, until I left his bed.

- *L. Figueroa*

Young Love

Memories don't play back to back anymore.
I had to figure out some things, just to be sure.
Don't be upset when you see this,
there's some things I had to get off my chest.

Baby, please don't be offended,
& don't go regretting all you did.
It was real, everything you feel.

I thought I really felt the same way you did.
I was wrong about a lot, I have to admit.
I adored you, I swear to you. I still do.
But I realized there's a difference between
wanting you, and just wanting
someone to talk to.

- L. Figueroa

Waking Up

So many arguments, it's enough to call it quits. I know you're tired of
me accusing, but you've left trails open for assuming.

I can't say it was all your fault that so many problems existed.
But I can tell the roles have shifted. It seems like one of us always
wants a little more than the other.
I guess this is what happens to strong-minded lovers.

I know you wish someone would tell you why I'm so hard to
understand, or why I pull away now when you reach for my hand.

Maybe we loved each other too much,
maybe we were always moving in a rush.

We never learned everything there was to know because we always
tried for a bit, and then let it all go. And you say you're not the way
you used to be, telling me there's a lot of new things I need to see.

But I always knew you better, I said I loved you in that letter,
assuming it would last forever, remember?

- L. Figueroa

Lucid Dreams

I had them often.

Depicted visions, but the explanation was missing.
Unfamiliar places with such strongly detailed faces,
why would anyone fake this?

There was always something next to me & it wouldn't let me sleep.
It was loud and aggressive with a terrifying message.
With evil eyes distorted, and a body so morbid.
"No mercy left for you kid."

An unprotected soul, with a body turning cold,
there was nowhere left to go. Reluctant to the agony,
"why is it so mad at me?"

I could never move, but I always felt myself screaming,
never realizing, I was only dreaming about the lies I was believing.

- *L. Figueroa*

Lesson Learned

The biggest mistake I made was loving **boys**.

They weren't bad people,

but they weren't ready for my love yet.

They were not **men** yet.

- L. Figueroa

Long Time Coming

I lay here, but I know I cannot stay here.
Choosing to believe the magic, charm, and front.
The empty truths, and covered up stunts.
What is the excuse this time? Does it rhyme too?
You'll do whatever it takes to make me *believe* you.
Until I'm calmed and my guard falls down, you go
around making me feel foolish and regretful, claiming
you're sorry you're so "forgetful".
But the problem is not you; it's me.
I can't allow myself to **hate**, when I am so *loving*.
So caring and kind, I swear I'm not blind.
I just can't give up on someone who holds
such a huge part of my own heart.
Your ability to make me forgive you is so scary.
I'm ashamed, but I'm not to be blamed.
Women love hard and passionately.
There's nothing more that I can explain, or get you to see.
Usually, the love I release is produced so freely,
but as of lately, there is none left in me.
And I hate that so much time flies
with such slow replies, but I've realized
there is no comfort left in your lies,
so I guess this is *goodbye*.

- L. Figueroa

Gracefully, she said:

I've got more important things to do,
than to sit around & worry about you.

- L. Figueroa

This Is Real

It comes in wild waves, sometimes low tides.
The motions of darkness vary each time.
People claim they know what depression is like,
but I have yet to find an accurate depiction of what its been for me.
Especially on the days when I can't seem to breathe.

It's not about the sky seeming "gray" or being sad for "no reason". It's about drowning, even though you know how to swim, and wanting a brighter light because yours is always dim.

The thing about depression is that it *leaves* then **comes back**.
It's a control over your spirit that throws you off track.
We try to act like everything will be okay, while the darkness stares at us with this conniving face. Laughing at our efforts to pray it away.

Depressed are the ones who laugh the hardest, so most of the time you wouldn't even know; this feeling lingers in spaces that don't show.
Wishing we could be happy again like the warm, and welcoming faces we admire. Having a purpose in life, is all that we desire.

A breath of fresh air would be nice, once in a while - she cried, with a smile.

- *L. Figueroa*

The Cycle

It just sucks you know? The emptiness.
Being in a relationship you loved
and never wanting anything to go wrong,
but the other person couldn't get it together
forcing you to move on, so you could love yourself.

Then you find someone else and you think they're *the one,*
and everything is perfect until they stop trying.

Now they're comfortable and you're hopeless.
Thinking it's all your fault & maybe it is
because you couldn't choose a good guy,
but how were you to know that it wouldn't work?
They always seem perfect at **first** anyway.

It's like they all know exactly what a girl wants
until they get the girl, and then forget how to treat her.
As if she's wrong to expect - what he's already proven
he can provide. The whole thing blows my mind,

because there you are sitting, trying to figure out what to say to make it feel okay, or express what you feel to only have him hear you & not listen, to say sorry but do it **again**.

To make you feel like you're the problem without actually saying *that* directly.
So you reconsider saying anything at all,
but then what are you left with...the emptiness.
And it just sucks you know?

- L. Figueroa

Mind Games

I guess old habits never die,

because you've got that same look in your eyes.

I always believe I know what you're thinking

but the truth only seems to come out when we're **drinking**.

This version of you that seems so damn charming.

I must say, its alarming.

Your tidal waves of affection, feel like perfection

until we reach the ends of your erection,

making room for that slim chance of rejection

to creep back in the picture.

What do I mean? *Never mind.*

Just pass me some more liquor.

- L. Figueroa

Time Wasted

From strangers to lovers,
then we turn into *just* friends.
But the excitement has died down,
just as fast as it began.
So now we're right back
to being strangers, *yet again*.

\- L. Figueroa

Never Cared

It's always something, isn't it?
A problem, an issue, an **excuse**.
You never notice the things you do.
"Get it together or forget me forever"
is a quote that lingers in my mind all the time.
But of course, love is blind.
I have never been the type of girl
to deal with this kind of stress
so consecutively.

Look at this *mess* you've made of me.

You're toxic,
and I'm home sick,
so we both won't quit.

I should know better but
when we're together…
It's like I'm under a spell,

until I realize I'm actually in hell.
And though you seemed heaven-sent,
I've realized our time together is irrelevant.
It isn't worth the frustration and agitation you bring me
with your bad habits and "forgetfulness".
I deserve better than *this*.

So let me go now, I'll find my way somehow.
You'll probably find another girl to bring back to your place,
and move at the same pace you did with me.
Just remind her that I am someone she could *never* be.

- L. Figueroa

Save Her

The disgust you leave behind is an acquired taste.
To know that, and still want more, is such a waste.

No scars painted upon your arms,
your heart is just fine.
Meanwhile this girl is left blind.
You stand selfish and guarded,
while she lets her walls down;
you just disregard it.

Men like you were meant to have daughters,
so you can learn how to treat women.
Love them openly and willing,
without the selfish attitudes
and bad decisions.

If your baby girl wakes up one day,
and asks you *why* she has to feel this way,
have you considered what you'll say?
I hope by then you understand,
that women should be treated better
never to be taken for granted or left damaged.
I hope that you see karma for what it is;
the pain that you've instilled in your kids.

- L. Figueroa

Loudest Fears

Confidence and doubt, insecurities and pride.

She had it all, *that* she couldn't hide.

A wandering soul, so beautiful, but so alone.

She has learned to be independent, & she has grown.

Believe that she has shown, that no one could ever truly

deter her from her destiny and all that she was meant to be.

But until then, she's been misled. Looking in her mirror,

asking how could someone, so full of life, feel so dead?

Why can't she look in that same mirror and see what I see?

The most genuine set of eyes looking back at me.

It's been a while since she's laughed, and felt the same.

The way she once felt before the betrayal and shame.

The emptiness has overpowered and it just seems to grow louder.

But don't undermine how her redemption will suffice one day.

When it does, I bet you won't know what to say.

- L. Figueroa

October

You'd be surprised at how much I compromise.
Covering up what I really feel inside.
There's something about wanting more than what we have,
"exceeding".
And we've obtained this bad habit of needing
people even though we don't want to be needed.

When you and I met,
I knew in my heart this would bring me pain.
I felt how strong my emotions would become
since the moment you said my name.
The thing about you is that, you've got so much.
I felt it in your touch.

You're probably still afraid of me
when I have the best intentions for you, in reality.
I know people like us don't come around often.
We don't like to be hurt, so we hide.
We don't like to give too much; it's something called *pride*.
But you said you were aware that a girl like me is rare.
And I told you I wasn't going anywhere,
so for you to leave me hanging like this,
just isn't fair.

- *L. Figueroa*

Fed Up

He said, "I wanna get involved with you".
See the world in the same ways you do.
I was searching for someone, and *he knew*.

But "I'm just not ready".
Damn, those words are heavy.

I heard that plenty of times,
but it always blows my mind,
as if it's the very *first* time.

Why do you men all use the same line?
Who gave you the right to waste my time?

I'll never understand.

Next one better take his memories with him,
because I truly don't want them.

- L. Figueroa

When You Call

My heart still jumps for you,
forgetting it's been split in two.
My stomach forms knots,
at the same weight of rocks.
My feet forget their responsibility.
Yet, I still run to you, so willingly.

Lovers are often blinded &
they don't seem to mind it.
I think it's because we all know
it feels better than being alone.

- L. Figueroa

Sebastian

He was a drug, my favorite addiction.
He was temptation, but he was medicine.
I wanted all of him.
He didn't refer to me as "gorgeous" or "pretty".
He used my name when he spoke to me.
Because to him, I was Lianne Marie,
and that felt better than anything.

- L. Figueroa

Gentle & Beautiful

Gentle soul, you're exhausted and it shows.
Gentle soul, don't let his fictional
representations taint your mental health.
Try not to fight the battle of proving yourself.
If you gave him the chance, he'll ruin all of you,
just 'cause you're *beautiful*.

Boys: they'll take all your love away,
because feelings switch from night to day.

Innocent and faithful, you are.
Gentle woman, you're a blessing, by far.
Know that not everything you see is what it seems.
Know that imagery can get messy.
Don't be weary, just let go and be free.
None of this is worth your *wasted* energy.

- L. Figueroa

Don't Fall For It

Used to have dreams that he was up to no good,
because he was.
Now you're having dreams that he misses you,
because he does.

- L. Figueroa

Who Would've Thought

They say tragedies take place in threes.
I just assumed all things deserved to be
set **free**, eventually.

One of the prettiest things that seems to scare me,
is realizing how one of your closest friends
could also be your enemy.

Mastering the ability to pretend
without really noticing it until the end.

Yeah, I think about it every now and then.

- L. Figueroa

Protect Your Peace

I'm trying to write something new.
Something that might only speak to a few
   This is far different from my usual.

I won't write about relationships this time,
or present lost love in the form of a crime.
I'm only trying to open your mind, the same
way I opened *mine*.

I always thought people appreciated the things
they claimed to like about someone, never
assuming they would cling onto someone
just for fun. Disappearing once they've realized
you're strong all on your own. As if it's unheard of
to walk alone.

But do me a favor?

Don't ever feel bad for sticking to your word,
& don't be quiet, when you want to be heard.

One day they'll be mad that you made it.
You can bet they were hoping that you'd quit.

Just know, you'll have haters wherever you go.
You better shine, no matter what though.

- *L. Figueroa*

The Interlude

My heart hurts from the pain I feel inside, sometimes. Pressured to let it go, but to also remain true to what I believe in. Never give up - this is what I believe in. This is the ground upon which I was raised. Follow your heart - go after what you want in life. But I wanted him, and I can't have him anymore. *"So let him go"*. Don't speak about him, don't think about him, teach yourself to forget about all the time you spent with him. This shit is *hard*. I should be focused on so many other things, but I'm a lover. How can someone like me, so intelligent and full of life, feel so lost at my prime? I am letting him go. So, why is he still on my mind? I don't understand, because in class they teach you about math and science, but nothing about social struggles and heartaches. I am convinced that everyone is too comfortable with disappointment in this generation. As women, we are expected to let boys disappoint us. We are taught to believe that "boys will be boys" and there is nothing more to it. They'll lie and most of the time, they'll give up on us once they get bored and search for someone better. We are taught that if we are smart enough to love ourselves, then we should not dwell on this pain, we have to remember that they have lost, and we have gained. We must have self-control over our emotions. We must walk away, thick-skinned and less willing to let love back in. But, I am smart. Smart enough to know that if I lose my sensitivity and ability to be compassionate, to protect my heart, I will jeopardize my sense of self. These solutions do not work for me, they do not coexist with my beliefs. I would have to change, who I am, to become heartless like the rest of you... and that is not something I want to do.

Dear Artists,

I am sure that you have learned as well as I have, that for someone to consistently produce something of substance requires a significant amount of skills. To create something *real*. Something that makes you feel, or something to help you heal. Whatever it is, there's a goal one must fulfill. As a writer, my job is to move you with my words, and stimulate your mind with the clarity it deserves. Yes, my experiences are mine, but if I can get you to relate through a couple of rhymes then I have mastered the craft of poetry, or *so it seems*. My only desire is to grab your attention through a time of deep reflection. And if in the process, I capture your heart then I have shed light in the dark. After all, what is life without **Art**?

Don't ever lose sight of your passion.

Yours Truly,

- L. Figueroa

Anxious

A person won't tell you right away,
that they never planned to stay.
No one ever wants to be blamed
for their own mistakes, or the pain
they may soon cause. I mean, would you
want to be reminded of your own flaws?

I guess common sense isn't so common.
This is the fifth time we've been on this.
People won't tell you how they play
the games they play. Honey,
that's a dead giveaway.

Soon my love, you will learn
the difference between feeling
warm, and getting **burned**.

And once you do,
I hope you remember all
that you've been through.

It takes a strong one to overcome
a lot of life's toughest lessons.
I hope this answers your questions.

- L. Figueroa

Soulmates

There's something about the way
you call me baby that melts my heart.
I've heard it a million times, and it's not a new word,
but the way you say it is *different*.
You don't say it to get your way.
You don't use it as a pet name,
or because you can't remember mine.
When you call me baby, I feel equal to you, and
somehow more loved than I have ever been.
When *you call me* baby, I feel like it's the best
word that's ever been spoken.

It's almost like Déjà vu; God told me it'd be you.
I didn't understand at first, but once we met, *I knew.*

Who better for me, than you?
I haven't got the slightest clue.

- L. Figueroa

A Different World

I want a love like Whitley & Dwayne.
No limits, no games ; no secrets & no shame.
I want a fresh kind of love, not a Kim K
& Mr. West kind of love. Stay well dressed to
impress kind of love. Let's make a statement with
our love, not just on and off dating 'cause we messed up.
Let's take our relationship to its greatest heights, till I'm
walking toward the altar dressed in all white, because
you're the only one in my sight. Growing old together
should be more than just a vision, and if you're ready
I'm more than willing. Let's be role models for this generation. Prove
that healthy love requires trust and communication. Support each
other to further our education, and applaud one another for our
invested dedication. I want a love that's kind and patient, but I'm still
waiting.

- *L. Figueroa*

Remember This

We retrace our steps through memories, too often.

Allowing ourselves to remember familiar faces,

and certain places that don't deserve

to take up space in our hearts anymore.

Not everyone is meant to grow with you.

- L. Figueroa

Disconnect

"**He doesn't listen**"

"**She doesn't get it**"

But you didn't communicate.
You yelled.
You assumed.
You cursed.
But you didn't communicate.
And that's the *difference*.

- L. Figueroa

The Irony

I think about letting go, all the time.
I have to let go of the way you smell,
the things I know you'd find funny,
the love I still...

I have to deal with the fact that someone
else loves me, the same way I love you.
And that person doesn't want to let me go,
which breaks my heart all over again,
because none of us will ever feel the same
way about each other. So what do we do?

- L. Figueroa

No Subs

Guilty minds will always believe
that every piece I've written is about *just* them.
Not realizing that **more** than one person
has done what they've done, to me.
Not understanding that this isn't hate mail.
This is a thank you.

It's true,
I have grown *because* of you.

- L. Figueroa

Selfish Love

I wish I knew how to say this poetically, but I can't.
If I state all my points steadily, I'll just rant.
I hate that almost every person I know
associates being in love with having control.
They either lose themselves in their lover
or they believe they should be a possession of the other.

Listen to me,
you do not belong to anyone.
You do not *need* to be tied down,
while you're still so young.

You may choose to share the love in your heart, but
that does not make someone else your counterpart.
Healthy love allows you to be yourself, but better.
And real love does not crack under pressure.
So how much you love, should not be measured.

- L. Figueroa

They asked;

"What makes you any different?"

Everything I put out into the world, is **real**.

My energy.
My words.
My friendship.
My love.

"So?"

Real will always recognize real.

- L. Figueroa

In This Generation

I wish you wanted me, like that drink you crave at 1:00 am.
I wish you looked for me, just like the girls who slide in your Dm's.
I wish you carefully set your lips on me, the same way you do your blunts.
I wish you treasured me like the new sneakers you like to flaunt.
I wish you studied me, the way you study new beats and rhymes.
I wish you read carefully through these lines.
I wish you knew me the way you know Chance lyrics.
I wish you listened to me, instead of saying you don't want to hear it.
I wish you considered my feelings as carefully as you consider your captions.
I wish you chose *me*, instead of wishing you had more options.

- L. Figueroa

Broken

I remember when they all tried saving
what was left of me, but I just wasn't ready.
I couldn't be.

I was confused,
how could one be happy after continuously
being stripped of the only things they knew to be real
& then be expected to heal?
Each and every time,
my mind was forced to press **restart.**
I had to empty out all of the love from my heart.

When people move on, they expect you to do so, too.
Change your way of being, just to make it through.
But that was never what I agreed to do.

- L. Figueroa

Noise

The anxiety can be so paralyzing some days.
Only my eyes can share the words I can't say.
Imagine losing your sense of direction.
Not being able to speak.
You call it being weak.
But imagine losing your tongue.
No one asks questions, anymore.
They just say "she's **numb**".

- L. Figueroa

Road to Recovery

The ability to laugh again, feels heavenly.
To smile openly, is my favorite remedy.
This harmony within me, it's shining steadily.
It's hard letting go, but I realized I don't need the negativity.

They say time heals all, and I swear I'm more than ready.
No one can take away all that I've built myself to be.
This heart within me, so genuine and pure, is not yours anymore.

You said you were done, and I agree. I need to take better care of me.
Don't feel bad for setting me free, I could not be more *lucky*. I'm so
thrilled to begin this new journey, because my vision is no longer
blurry. The tears are done falling, and my happiness is the only thing
calling. I am always reminded to keep my head up, and stop wasting
time being fed up.

I can't wait for these wounds to heal entirely, and they'll do so *quietly*.
But my recovery will be the loudest thing you hear from me. With no
words, at all, you'll realized I've gotten better. And sadly, all you'll
have left is this letter.

- *L. Figueroa*

To you,

So many times, I reread my work and ask myself,
if I'm sure this is what I want to show the world.
This side of me, so vulnerable, and now open to criticism.
Knowing I probably won't accept much of it lightly,
and not all of you will agree with every word you see.

There are hundreds of poets, millions of writers,
and so many more critics. *Am I ready for this?*

There are so many forms of poetry, and literature.
There are so many different types of books,
believe me *I know*.

Why would mine stand out?

Because no matter who you are, or where you come from,
pain is pain, and love is love. You've felt it before or it's coming.
And my words will assure you that we are on the same page. We are
thinking the same thoughts. Pain hurts, and love heals. No matter
which one we experience more of, we still grow.

So I'm asking you to grow with me, grow through me.
And to some of you, grow for me.

Love Always,
L. Figueroa

If I Ever Said I love You, I Meant It

I'll always want the best for you,
even if that means a future without me.

It frightens me how things can end so easily,
but I have learned that we must take these lessons openly.
You are someone I will always keep close to my heart,
no matter how far apart.
Our laughs and dreams were shared for a reason,
even if only for a few seasons.

I will always remember that.

And if I ever see you in passing,
just remember I always had your back.

\- *L. Figueroa*

Like Mother, Like Daughter

My mother didn't like to be needed by us.
I think it was because she was never
really allowed to need anyone else, herself.
I wondered where her frustration stemmed from
each time I asked for help. But it wasn't until
my twenties that I realized her problem wasn't
extending love. Her problem was not having
received enough of it. She lacked guidance on how
to love us because she lacked the kind of love
she deserved her whole life.

*You deserve so much more than you've been given,
and I won't settle until I know you are truly happy.*

- L. Figueroa

Listen

Keep saying it will all be okay,
my visions blurred & I don't believe a word you say.
Silence
I try and reach out to you,
touch your hand, once or twice, but you feel so indecisive.
Silence
Why can't you just let me know what you're feeling?
It's clear we both need some healing.
But you're so closed off, and misleading.
Silence
I'm so confused, feeling used, my emotions I let you abuse, with
silence.

- L. Figueroa

Soft Spot

Absence makes the heart grow fonder they say,
as if they know I'm missing you.
It must be painted in the reflection of my eyes,
because in all my day dreams, I'm kissing you.
I get lost in your charming ways.
I know I remind you all the time,
but you're the fuel on my slowest days.
You're my warmth and safety
beyond the damp and rainy haze;
my clarity for the messes I've already made.
I am so clumsy, how can you want me?
You are so smooth and elegant
while I am so soft and sensitive.
Don't be fooled by my admiration for you,
I am in love with me *too*.
I am aware of the depth of my beauty
and my intelligence, and the power
of my own independence.
However, when I love,
I transition into a different version of myself.
Allowing my feelings to coexist at the sight
of your presence. It's not always safe,
I've learned the hard way. After all,
absence makes the heart grow fonder they say.

- *L. Figueroa*

Influenced

As young women we start to believe it is okay
to give parts of ourselves away.
As long as they aren't too big,
as long as it doesn't mean *too* much.
But what's the rush?
It shouldn't be so easy for some guy to get your number,
or your conversation, while he keeps you waiting.
It should not be that easy for you to surrender your loyalty,
before a guy has proven that you should be treated like royalty.
When you give a guy too much, too fast, his efforts do not last.
Of course, this is not always the case, but more often than not, this is
what we face. As young women we start to believe it is okay.

- L. Figueroa

Dead Roses

There you go claiming you're tired of men,
even though I heard you and him are talking again.
You keep saying you're going to stop,
I just don't know when.
I could tell he's been lying
when I see you crying.
I'm not sure why you even keep trying.
But I know you're anticipating the correction of his behavior,
just so you guys can become something "major".
Yet, he's gone in the brain girl.
He's got another one of you, times two
'cause you *know* they come in waves, girl.
I wish you would eliminate yourself from this game.
It's clear you can't let go of the pain,
especially when someone mentions his name.
I know it's such a shame,
because these guys are all the same.

- L. Figueroa

Introvert

I am nothing like you –
I would not mix well with your crew.
I am quiet and awkward, and for some
reason or other, I am always bothered.
I get mad too easily over nothing serious.
I hate when people judge off of lack of experience.
Most of the time, I do my own thing. I stay out of the way.
A lot of times, you'll find that I have nothing to say.
People often misinterpret my need to be observant.
Assuming that I'm uninterested, or that my thoughts are limited.
But really, I am learning the vibes that surround me.
I don't open up to *just* anybody.

- L. Figueroa

My Turn

I always wondered why no one ever gave you a real chance.

They solely relied on a quick glance.

Something I did not understand.

You are a vision.

The kind I had always been missing.

I wondered what a relationship with you would be like, if it lasted.

There were so many reasons why I felt attracted.

I think that's why your ex's still check on you from time to time.

But that's irrelevant because I would give up anything to make you
mine. If they only knew, a life with you would be a dream come true.

The kind I would love to pursue.

- *L. Figueroa*

Loyal

I remember when the love of my life said,
"You're too good to be true. There is no way
you could be so beautiful, and be this faithful."

If only he knew…

I never wanted anyone else,
but it was up to him to see for himself.

- L. Figueroa

To My Little Sister,

*If there is anyone that I have grown to love more than myself, it is you.
I love you beyond words could ever explain, I would do whatever I
could, in seconds, just to prevent you from feeling any pain. I know
this is expected, because you are my sister, you're my blood and we
come from the same tribe. But not all sisterhoods survive; not all
females love each other with the same amount of pride. Regardless of
this, I want nothing more than to witness you flourish, beautifully into
the star you were destined to be. As your sister, I promise to always
watch your back, that's a guarantee. I know you don't feel like I
always understand you, but believe me I do. I was once in your shoes.
I've been heart broken, and betrayed too. I let a lot of insignificant
things get in the way of my focus. I tell you over and over, but I need
you to know this. I will do whatever I can to protect you from harm, I
would lie, if need be, to defend you from mom. I will always be the
shoulder you need to cry on, especially when the rest of your world
seems to be gone. We come from the same mother, so you and I will
always be like each other. I hope you never forget, no matter how
upset you might get. You are my heart, because of you each day I
strive to be better. The bond we share is something I'll treasure,*
forever.

Letters Undelivered

*Dedicated to my brother, whom is the reason
I started writing again. May he rest in peace.*

Dear Brandon,

Our baby sister is getting so big now.
Man, if you could see her, you'd be so proud.
She acts just like you used to.
She's like the female version of you.
It's been a few years now, and I don't even know how ;
all this time has passed by, and no one ever told us why.
Why they had to take you away, that heartbreaking day.
& she still talks about you, ya know?
There's *no way* we could ever let you go.
We agreed we'd give anything to have you back.
Now she's crying... and I just can't handle that.
We all told God it was too soon, but he told us that he needed *you.*
I told him to remind you that we miss you, our brothers and parents too.
And I know that we'll meet again, but try and be good until then.

With Love,

- L. Figueroa

83

To The Women I Love

While writing this book, I started to realize how strong and beautifully powerful you are, for never giving up. You are filled with wisdom, pride, strength, dedication, independence and so many more great and admirable character traits, but most people do not take the time to remind you how great you are. I am sorry that people don't, but we notice. I notice everyday in myself; the good and bad that comes from all the lessons you have done your best to teach me. But because many do not always show you how much they appreciate you, it can be upsetting from time to time. This is your reason. You start to believe that you are not as important as other things in life, but that is not true. Don't let it fool you. We would be *nothing* without you.

I think that I am very lucky. I am a lucky young lady to have such a beautiful support system, and such truly admirable women to lead me in life. You work so hard, and continuously set an amazing example of what a strong woman should be! When I was younger, teachers would ask me who my hero was, and who I believed was a strong female figure in my life, it was not until recently that I realized who it was all along. It was you, you have given me so much to be grateful of, so much to live up to. Thank you for molding me into the woman I am today.

For Grandma, Mom, Alba, Aurora, Evelyn, Marilyn, —

The Purpose

From our earliest days up until adulthood, we are often asked what we want to do with our life, or what we want to be when we grow up. Ever since I was a little girl, I would say "I want to help people". I listed any career that I believed did a good job of that. At the age of seven, I said I wanted to be a teacher so that I could teach others with passion and patience. At the age of seventeen, I said that I wanted to be a nurse, so that I could care for others with love, and nurture them the way I believed they needed to be taken care of. In college, I started to believe that I wanted to be a therapist, because I knew that I was meant to cure the minds and hearts of those around me, in some way. However, none of these careers truly fit me, none of them were what I really wanted to be. Now, if someone asked me why I wrote this book, I would say because I knew from a young age that I was meant to help people, or rather *heal* people. I care about others more than myself, which is why I know I would do my job well, no matter what it turned out to be. The thing about me is that I wholeheartedly care for anyone I cross paths with, in ways they don't even know they need at the time of meeting me. I know that every person needs to be loved, and reminded of how much better things will get regardless of the challenges they face in life. And for some reason or other, I always tend to meet people at a time when they need it most. I know, first hand, what it feels like to be broken, and how difficult things can be during those times. I have learned that I am better at helping others because healing others, helps *me*. It heals me, too. It provides me with a sense of purpose. Feeling is a gift, not a curse — I hope you understand this, if nothing else.

Pass this book along to whomever needs it.

Keep up with me on social media for more –

Twitter: @LettersToYoux
Facebook: @LettersToYoux
Instagram: @LettersUndelivered_

Letters Undelivered

Made in the USA
Middletown, DE
06 April 2017